Driving the Technical Sale

Winning over the technical influencers.

Lance Knight

outskirtspress
DENVER, COLORADO

Driving the Technical Sale
Winning over the technical influencers. Master the Evaluation process.
  Paving the way for expansion.

Cover image and author photo: Barton Wood

Outskirts Press, Inc.
http://www.outskirtspress.com

ISBN: 978-1-4787-7665-9

Outskirts Press and the "OP" logo are trademarks belonging to Outskirts Press, Inc.

PRINTED IN THE UNITED STATES OF AMERICA

Table of Contents

Foreword

When Lance and I first began selling software together in 2007, the proof-of-concept (POC) or pilot was just starting to become a universally required step in the enterprise sales cycle. We would lay the groundwork for the sale through meetings and demos, but risk-averse buyers were not pulling the trigger until their team was convinced that the solution would work for them. More often that not, this meant getting hands-on with the software and proving it themselves. Everyone was from Missouri: *Don't tell me, show me.* As a majority of prospects made the POC a mandatory part of their buying process, the question become *how do we optimize the POC process to ensure a good experience and guarantee a successful outcome, i.e., a closed deal?*

Our solution was to put intelligence and structure

around the POC process. As a software startup with limited resources, our first step was to determine which customers would benefit from a POC. We simply could not support running these for everyone in the pipeline, and our upfront qualification was to offer the POC to prospects that would 1) commit the necessary resources, and 2) agree to buy as a next step. We walked away from a number of companies who didn't agree to this. Once qualified, we worked to distill the proof points our customers needed down to a handful of criteria that we knew we could fulfill. These were written into the charter, and every action in the POC was designed to demonstrate how we could meet those proof points.

Our team moved with focus and military precision through the POC process. We had seen terrible results when sales teams simply let customers run amok in their platform, and we determined that upfront training and close support would be critical to ensure a positive experience and successful outcome. We scheduled regular checkpoint meetings to assess progress. We spent many hours on the phone answering questions and guiding the customer through the application. Most importantly, we kept the customer focused on their key proof points and how we would help them achieve these. Since we had agreed upfront that this proof would be rewarded with a sale, the mantra became: *show me how you'll meet my needs and I'll buy.* As we got better in the POC process, our win rate went from 25% to 90%. It was apparent that we had found a formula that really worked.

While process and structure certainly play a key part in closing the technical sale, the psychology behind the plan is just as important. We made the customer understand from the beginning that we had a plan. Our deliberate and ordered approach was apparent as we walked the customer through the checklist and created the charter. We gave the customer confidence in our abilities to deliver on the POC and the sense that we would be a good, long-term partner. Contrast this approach to our competitors who simply tossed the keys to the customer and told them to enjoy their test drive. Our POC approach often shut down competitive threats before they could gain momentum, and there were countless examples of customers who chose not to run a parallel process with competitors once they engaged with us.

The connection between the sales engineer and the evaluation team also became a key driver to achieving a successful outcome. As SE, Lance was the Sherpa who would guide the customer up the mountain. With this level of personal attention, we were able to validate each proof point in the charter, which led to very strong relationships. As an expert, Lance brought credibility to the process and customers trusted him. He made sure that the customer *wanted* our solution, and that we would be the recommended solution when it came time to make a decision. While the salesperson needs to drive the commercial terms and have the tough conversation, the SE can be a friend and mentor who pulls the customer aside and whispers *I want to make you look good. Count on me to do whatever it takes.*

You will be amazed at the results that this process generates for you and its immediate impact. You will blow away the competition and impress the hell out of your customers. At the end of the day, any POC worth doing is worth doing well, and when you approach these with a plan, you put yourself in the best position possible to win the deal. Good luck and good selling.

Jonathan Jewett
SVP Sales

About the Author

The ability to not only see the big picture but also bring it to fruition is both rare, and only gained with years of experience. This is what Lance Knight brings to the table.

Calling on years of business experience, Lance has, at one time or another, been called the following: top-performing, executive-level, software sales professional, corporate project manager, entrepreneur, software developer, and corporate marketing manager. His specialty lies in the ability to conceptualize what's needed on a large scale, and then lead the project to a successful conclusion. His skill for successfully bridging the gap between solutions and technology brings a decidedly left and right brain approach. Lance's teams have been involved in selling over one-hundred million dollars' worth of software

over his career. Lance is more than a salesperson—
he is a sales engineer who understands the twists and
turns that any sales opportunity can take. He has also
spent hours understanding the international and do-
mestic market, which helps him to create frameworks
for continued success for companies.

An entrepreneur's entrepreneur, Lance has
launched several successful companies, and always
seems to be in three places at once. This is a testa-
ment to his understanding of very different aspects of
corporate structure—he is as at home in the IT depart-
ment as he is in the highest-level sales meeting.

1
What's Changed and Why

Anybody who has been in the software business for more than just a few years can no doubt remember how things used to work back in the "old days" (which really wasn't all that long ago). Back in the early 2000s, in the wake of the dot.com collapse and the emergence of SaaS, an entirely new sales landscape was just beginning to emerge. Product evaluations or POCs were rare, and when they did happen they were almost always paid. Keep in mind that downloading software was not that easy, so there were far more technical hurdles than today. Of course, the changes in the industry weren't all the result of technological advancements. Financial factors played a significant role as well. The booming 1990s economy fell precipitously toward the end of that decade, and companies were not spending money as freely as they once did. If they were going to buy something new, they wanted to first justify the expenditure. This shift took place after the initial downturn in the tech industry as the dot-coms went away and the potential menace of Y2K fizzled.

The thinking among those procuring software became "prove it to me." Complicating the picture even more, most companies have already seen your product online and know what you do and how you do it before they even call you. That makes the dynamics of the sales cycle completely different than it was back in the 80s and 90s where salespeople had to go out and find clients. Now it's been reversed and they find you. They take the initiative, find your company, download the software, and then buy it

I can't overstate how significant this change is, even in other industries. Think about the car business. Back in the 1980s nobody knew how much a car was, what the retail sticker was, invoice, buy back, and other factors. Flash-forward to today, however, and everybody knows what all of those things are thanks to all the information available on the Internet.

The information revolution marked the beginning of a whole new ballgame for both buyers and sellers. If I'm a seller, I can find out anything that I need to know about the individual that I'm working with by checking them out on sites such as Facebook or LinkedIn. It also greatly helps the buyers because now they know what you do and what your company does well in advance of you ever even making a pitch. Once upon a time the typical salesperson was a guy with a Rolodex and a book and all of these services to offer. He called on customers and formed relationships with them. The concept of "relationship selling" became critically important. Then things started to shift in the late 1990s and early 2000s when companies gained the ability to go out and find products and services much more easily than ever before. They could now very easily do some research and find out about a product before having any contact with a salesman.

For sellers, one of the practical consequences of all these changes was that we were no longer selling solutions after highlighting problems, which was how it had always been before. In this new environment, the buyer came to us already knowing both the problem and the solution, and called us specifically for that solution. This meant that modern era salespeople need to be far more knowledgeable than they had been in the past. It's now much harder to tell customers things that they don't already know. That means salespeople in this era must be equipped to bring more and better business recommendations than ever before.

Moreover, with the ubiquity of open source technology, downloading software and trying it for free before buying it, sellers had to find new ways to deal with the rapidly evolving environment. This easy delivery of the product naturally led to customers saying, "Well, let me try it out first. I want you to prove to me that this is the right product for our company. But for the seller, it had to be more than just putting the software out there and letting prospective buyers tinker with it. There needed to be a codified process that guided the customer through the evaluation or POC.

Initially, this was not a good development for us, as most of the members of our sales team had no experience in doing business this way. In a very real sense, training them in this new approach was like a person learning to walk or ride a bike for the first time. They were used to simply coming in, showing a product, and moving through the sales cycle. Then, when customers began asking about doing a pilot, the salespeople would say, sure, and simply send them the software by email so they could check it out.

Well, it didn't take long before we realized how incredibly shortsighted that was as a way of doing business. Indeed, it was wholly inadequate for dealing with the realities of marketing software in the twenty-first century. That's because, without a systematic approach attached to the trial period, it wasn't in anyway a true pilot at all. As a result, we saw significantly lengthened sales cycles while customers were trying out the software. Moreover, it was not the priority of these individuals to be examining it on any given day, and there was no codified schedule of meetings. In the past, there would always be a pretty fast sale cycle, usually based on the use of a demo. Now, however, the salespeople were engaging the buyers in a "pilot" where they were basically just saying, "Here's the software and a user name. Use it all you want."

But there were major flaws with this method. For one thing, the customer never really could be completely sure if the software was providing the solution for a specific problem because the customer wasn't given any guidance for evaluating the product. They were left to their own devices, which was the exact opposite of what the salesperson wanted. The customer needed to be educated on how to effectively evaluate the software so they could come to a business decision.

These early missteps not only fostered longer sales cycles, but they also resulted in declining sales. With no clearly defined process in place, a salesperson would often end up spending a lot of time with a prospect, but it was not productive time. It was not structured, and would frequently lead nowhere.

This really should not have surprised anyone. Customers typically don't know how to evaluate software on their own. Therefore, without education and guidance, many pilots would be doomed to fail. They end up just tinkering around with the software. More likely than not, they are not asking the right questions, and they probably aren't even sure what they are looking for. I remember when I used to hear salespeople say that they were letting customers self-evaluate and I would ask them what kind of results they were getting. They would usually tell me that the results actually weren't very good…but that was the method that everybody was using for selling software.

I realized that there had to be a better way. I knew that just throwing evaluations out there was pretty much a recipe for disaster. Without asking the right questions and engaging the customers on a more meaningful level, it was a lot like simply putting our product out there and then crossing our fingers that they buy it. That's not a legitimate evaluation, and falls far short of a bona fide sales effort. We needed to start asking questions like, "What do you want to prove?" and "What do you want to see?" We could then competently utilize the evaluation process as a golden opportunity to do solution selling.

The key is building a solution for the customer ahead of time, and then presenting it to them. These days, the customer usually already knows what you have to sell, which is why I firmly believe that solution selling has now shifted to evaluations, i.e., the POC stage. Once you have a process in place, although each customer is somewhat unique and wants to do things differently over time, for the most part the methods that work for one evaluation will work for other pilots as well. That's part of the beauty of our system; every facet of it does not have to be custom-tailored for each individual customer. We would keep track of what we learned from one evaluation to the next, and that information would prove invaluable as we refined our techniques and perfected the processes that we had in place for our evaluation. Some customers, for example, might want to test the product in their own environment, where others may simply have something finite that they want to prove.

The point is that you need to be having periodic meetings with the customer during the pilot, so that you can make sure that you understand their perspective as precisely as possible. Simply saying, "Here's the software, go try it out," as we came to clearly came to understand, was never going to lead to large-scale success for any salesforce trying to sell to businesses. On the contrary, we would implement an evaluation charter, which was a plan that we would put together that would show to a customer in exacting detail how they would evaluate the software, and the meetings we would have with them. The most productive of these are what I call "deep dive" meetings, because they involve getting on the phone with the evaluator and presenting to them additional information about the product that was previously unknown to them. (Solution selling)

With evaluations, the salesperson should be guiding the customer to these deeper levels based on the charter. For example, let's say you wanted to evaluate a word processor. If it's one of the better ones, it will have lots of features that support a number of very useful functions. There are certain things that a user wants to do, but they may not just come right out and say it. People are rarely as articulate and precise as we would like for them to be. That is why we would schedule a deep dive meeting to highlight those capabilities of the software that you want to stand out. This would be based on what the customer told us they were really looking for, and we would take the initiative and explore those aspects of the product in depth, emphasizing the solutions that the product has to offer.

Here is something else to consider: the evaluation process itself helps to qualify prospective buyers. For instance, if we go to a customer and we request that they fill out a questionnaire, but they are reluctant and say, "We just want to try it (the software) out," that's a strong indication that they really haven't thought it through. This may prompt us to walk away, if it turns out that we would be wasting valuable time with a customer that is very unlikely to become a closed sale.

We tell customers right up front that as part of the evaluations we want to schedule these deep dive meetings to truly educate them about the software so that they can make an informed buying decision. This leads to an added benefit (for the seller). It goes beyond the fact that the buyers appreciate our technology and how we present it. When they see how much thought we have put into the pilot, and the superiority of our methodology and our processes, they feel confident that we're probably going to be as trustworthy and professional in the post-sales environment as we were during the sales phase. This leads to repeat customers, in large part because we addressed all the value points that they had identified for us when we first initiated the evaluation.

2

The New Approach

The changing conditions of the economy and of the software industry have necessitated an entirely new approach when it comes to the use of pilots and evaluations. The process can be broken into three distinct steps: prepare, prove, and close. In subsequent chapters we will examine each of these in much more detail. For now, you just need to know the basics. When it comes to the prepare phase, there is a great deal of work to be done to set the stage for a successful evaluation. We are asking a whole lot of questions right from the start, so that we know exactly what the customer should be looking for. As you will soon see, this is crucial in order for the entire process to even get started.

Also as part of the prepare phase, we will compose the charter, which is an action plan for how all of the teams involved in the evaluation will work together. It is essentially a project plan that serves a number of functions, including allowing the evaluator and assistant to work together more closely.

Earlier we had alluded to asking numerous questions. These come about by way of a questionnaire, which is designed to not only gather information, but to spot any red flags that may arise. The answers that you receive on this questionnaire will provide invaluable insights into precisely what it is that the customer needs to test for in the product through this evaluation.

In the prove stage, you are executing on the charter. You are having the meetings that have been scheduled in the charter and you're setting up "deep dive" meetings (more on that later) to try to really get to the heart of certain issues.

The close phase, of course, is where you build upon everything that you've worked so hard to establish in the first two phases in order to finalize the sale. It too needs to be done in a precise, guarded manner in order to bring the entire process to a successful conclusion.

This new approach is already working for professionals in the real world. Jamie Wetzel has been in the software business since 1999 and has been involved with pilots that entire time. He has been utilizing the strategy for about two years now, and has seen tremendous results from it. A lot has changed over the years, of course, especially with the new generation that has been brought up with the prolific usage of mobile devices. But when he first started out in sales it was much easier to control things and steer everything in a certain direction, because back then customers did not have at their fingertips (online) the vast amounts of information that are readily available and easily accessible today. Today, people already have 80% of the information that they need before even calling the vendor for the very first time. With the Internet and the widespread availability of information and details, people contact you after they have already done a lot of preliminary work. As a result they tend to have a less obvious, more open willingness to allow the vendor to lead them through the process.

The bad news is that this can make life harder for a salesperson. Think about how most of us typically use our mobile devices today. With a few taps of our fingers we can download an app, install it, let it self-configure, and then try it out all in the time it takes to go through your local drive-thru. And if we don't like it we simply delete it. That same kind of mindset has crept into the thinking of the personnel who are tasked with investigating and trying out, and then making recommendations and decisions on software. They, in a very real sense, view major purchases in the same way that they consider small and relatively inconsequential software downloads.

The good news is that using the proper sales protocols and techniques, you can instill in your clients a new way of looking at things. This is the new approach mentioned in the chapter title. It involves being more succinct and making sure that your evaluation is more guided and not just something that the customer "feels their way" through on their own. The days of doing business that way are over...unless steady, brisk sales are not important to you.

As part of this new approach you need to help customers reframe and reshape their mindset in such a way that they realize that what you are offering them is not just some small, little app. Rather, it is something that is important and critical for a major business entity.

It all starts by engaging the people who are in higher-up positions, the ones that the people who are directly involved in the pilot will be reporting to. These are the ones who will ultimately be making the final decisions when it comes to purchasing. These stakeholders will be receiving the recommendations that come as a result of the pilot, so it is crucial to engage them in the process as early on as possible. We want to get them involved and participating in the conversation in a way that makes them realize that doing so will be an efficient use of their time and make their life easier. It is imperative to show them how they are going to *directly and personally* benefit from your product.

Jamie has also found it very helpful to get involved with the "solutions engineer" at the prospect's company very early on in the process as well. In fact, he says that it is critical. In the past, this individual would be treated as a "wrench in a toolbox" that could be pulled out when needed and then put back. However, by personalizing the process and making sure that the solutions engineer is involved in the sale itself, we are doubling down in our efforts to guide the customer toward their target objective.

Like other sales professionals, Jamie agrees that it is essential to be very systematic when it comes to approaching evaluations. "What are we trying to accomplish, and what steps do we need to take to accomplish that?" is the key question that anchors his entire strategy. This way, rather than just letting prospective customers "kick the tires," you are helping them to identify a specific set of items that you can help them execute. This helps them understand the business benefits to both the person doing the evaluation and the company as a whole.

Keep in mind that customers typically have no idea how to evaluate new products. They are looking for someone to help show them how to evaluate it. In essence, we are giving them a process to know what exactly they should be evaluating for, and how to be more succinct in coming to conclusions. It is our job to guide them into knowing what they should be looking for. If they don't know what they want, it's our job to come in and tell them both what they want and how to convince their boss that our software is the solution they are looking for.

It all begins by giving the customer a framework in which to evaluate. That means sharing with them a process that will help them move forward in their evaluation more quickly. They may have in mind that they want to go ahead with a pilot before making any decisions, but they are generally ambiguous about what that evaluation will entail. One of the best things that we can do is to shift their thinking from the abstract to the concrete. The framework that we help them put in place is highly detail oriented. This framework is more or less the same for all customers, though the use cases are likely to be customized.

It all begins with having the customers fill out a questionnaire. This helps to ensure that nothing about the process is haphazard or random in any way. On the contrary, it is guided very carefully and purposefully, and the questionnaire is a key component for setting the stage appropriately. It serves as your first "gatekeeper" when it comes to the qualifications of the prospect to evaluate your software. There are certain red flags to be on the lookout for, i.e., if in the questionnaire they say things that are far off from what you do, right away you will know that this is a low-quality, low-qualified opportunity. If they say things that will take a long time to prove, then that will give you a better understanding of the time commitment, thereby improving the accuracy of your pipeline. That is why we consider the questionnaire to be the first step in helping both the customer and your salespeople accurately forecast when a sale will be made.

I prefer to try to limit all of the questions to one page, though I know there are some companies that extend it to two pages. We usually email the questionnaire to the customer. Then they fill it out and afterwards we make a visit to their office and review the responses with them in person. In going over these results with them, we can then figure out how to build an evaluation charter out of it.

This makes sense, as the first step in all sales work is asking the right questions. You learn to understand the customer's needs, and then figure out how you're going to deliver a great value to that customer.

3
Prepare

When it comes to running a successful pilot, you should never take shortcuts. Do things the right way from the very beginning. In fact, you need to be taking the right steps well in advance of that. It's not just about preparing the customer, however. More specifically, it's about preparing the customer for success. How? By making it as clear as possible to them what to expect, and letting them know in no uncertain terms that the evaluation process will have well defined goals. That way, when success is achieved it will be unmistakable and there will be no ambiguity about it.

It all starts with the questionnaire. I don't think it's possible to overstate the value of this crucial piece of the puzzle. Once I get it back after the customer has finished filling it out, the first thing that I need to do is an internal review, making sure that we can deliver what will be expected of us. Then we have a review with the customer, which is our opportunity to prepare and see things that the customer didn't necessarily know that they wanted to evaluate, but would be easy for us to evaluate for them.

We also at this preliminary stage of the process want to give them things that they need to do on their end. You go over every aspect of the evaluation charter with the customer and you all come to agreement about it upon completion. If there are any "tactical" items that the customer needs before they evaluate, you want to make sure that they go ahead and do all of that ahead of time before you begin the evaluation with them.

This would work in many sales situations, not just for software. Let's say that you want to evaluate a car. Test driving a car is in fact a demonstration. Certain preparations need to be made beforehand. For example, the salesperson has to be sure that the vehicle has gas in it before taking out a prospective customer on a test drive. Just imagine the predicament you'd be in by forgetting this one simple step!

Meanwhile, depending on the situation, the salesperson in charge of the pilot will have a meeting with others who will be involved in the evaluation process and determine precisely how they will engage that customer. This is called an internal review. They go over what they most likely can and cannot do with this particular customer and decide how they want to steer them and the next steps to take.

Next comes what is called an external review with the person who filled out the questionnaire. This is an excellent opportunity to continue filling out the document, as well as informing the customer about things that you can do that will be successful in the pilot. This helps you to better project your pipeline and allows the customer to learn exactly what it is that your company will or will not do. Or, it may turn out that you can tell the customer that what they are asking for is not something that can be done in an evaluation, but can be done in a deployment.

After all of the internal and external reviews have been completed and you've worked with your prospect, it's time to create what I call an evaluation charter. This is a project plan that sets up the "terms of engagement," as it were, of how you're going to help them to evaluate the software. It also puts a timeline in place for different meetings. What's most important is that it codifies the entire process. This is all designed to reduce the amount of time that it takes the customer to evaluate the product. It provides a logical process for the customer to determine if the product will fit their needs. It also gives you a very good snapshot of where things stand regarding the pipeline.

Each charter will have different dates and milestones, but the framework for building the charter is always pretty much the same. The charter may include things that you can't do in an evaluation, but are still part of the presentation in the sales cycle. This allows you to solution-sell to this customer during an evaluation.

For example, let's say you were buying a new bedroom set. One of the things you would want to see is, will this new bedroom set give me the comfort that I want for the next ten years? Well, let's think about how we could go about demonstrating that. You could in this example show the customers the craftsmanship that went into the bedroom set that will give it the longevity they are looking for. Remember, what you're selling are solutions, telling them about all of the qualities that went into the set's manufacture.

When it comes to a technical evaluation for a computer-related project, first you need to make sure the customer has a place where you can install the software. That may sound simplistic, but why take any chances? The last thing you would want to do would be to go out to their company to begin an evaluation, only to find out that they don't have anywhere to put the software. Moreover, if there are other parties who are going to be involved in the evaluation, you need to be certain that they will be there during your initial meeting. You also must be sure to have all of the proper permissions, clearances and access within the company to which you are selling your product or service.

Going back to the car example, you want to make sure that the customer has his or her spouse present, if that person is going to be an integral part of the evaluation and the decision about whether or not to purchase the new vehicle.

It's all about getting your ducks in a row – doing all of the necessary legwork well ahead a time. Far too often a sales professional is eager to go ahead and initiate an evaluation, only to find out that the prospective customer doesn't even have permission to install the software on the right server. As a result of this mishap you have damaged your own reputation because you did not take care of all of those details in advance. It makes you look less than professional.

Take every necessary precaution. For instance, if you're in the software world and your customer needs to download a large file, you want to make sure that they do that ahead of time. As everyone knows, there can often be problems when it comes to downloading large files. It could be a network issue, a problem with a server, or something else, so you want to be as proactive as possible in thinking through everything that could potentially slow your customer down, and prepare them for it. If you don't come right in and install the software with no problems, it immediately makes it look as if your product is confusing. Not to mention that it makes a terrible first impression. In our automobile example, just imagine if you took a car out from the dealership for a test drive and it ran out of gas! Yes, that would pretty much kill the deal right then and there.

A major part of the Pilot Engagement process is setting expectations about how you are going to perform. *We are going to this. You are going to that.* These are goals that you need to be sure to get into your charter. If you don't get these things written and included ahead of time, then the evaluation will never have a tangible conclusion, which, as far as I am concerned, is another way of saying that it has been a failure. It is crucial to always know precisely what it is that you are trying to achieve. Always have the end game in mind.

Let's return to that test drive scenario again (we should be ready to buy the darn thing by now!). Before we even begin to demo this new vehicle, there are certain things that we should already know. What is more important to the customer, fuel efficiency, or is it power that they want to see? Find out what is important for the people that you are selling to, and know what it is that they should be testing for. You're not only helping yourself by doing this, but you are undoubtedly helping them as well. By showing them what the car can do, and focusing on what is important to them, the evaluation has added value and is more meaningful than it would have been if you were concentrating on things that are relatively unimportant to the buyer.

You also need to determine what "deep dives" you are going to do. All of this is captured in writing and put down in the questionnaire so that both sides can agree upon it. This is all done up front, so that later when we come to the conclusion meeting we can point out all of the things that the customer was looking for initially and which have now been sufficiently proven to them. If it was the car-buying scenario, we would ask them, "So did we show you everything that you needed to see regarding fuel efficiency?" We want both parties on the same page. The expectations need to be aligned and free of any ambiguity.

Obviously, at no point (until money changes hands) can you get a guarantee that a prospect is going to become a paying customer, no matter how closely you adhere to the right steps. But you can get pretty close to that, by securing what I would call a "soft commitment." This is when they assure you that if you are able to prove A, B, and C to them, they will buy.

Interestingly enough, when setting up an evaluation a sales professional not only needs to be accommodating, but he or she also needs to know when it is prudent to instead (politely, of course) say no to certain requests. If our car customer had come to us and said, "OK, here's what I need. I want to take the car on a three-day trip for several thousand miles. Only then will I be able to know if it will truly suit my needs." Well, that would of course not be cost-effective or practical, so we would need to decline. It's really not much different in other evaluation situations, including software. They might say that they want to try it out for a year, put it into production, and find out if it can do all kinds of various tasks.

Your reply would have to be, "We appreciate that you would like to do that, but we're simply not geared up for that kind of thing." If you determine that what the customer is asking for is not in the best interests of your company, then you need to find a way to gently walk away. It is incumbent upon the sales professional to diplomatically let them know that you are anchored to established parameters, and there are in place certain boundaries that you will not cross.

It's also possible that they will ask for something that is an unreasonable expectation. If that car buyer, for example, wanted the biggest, heaviest vehicle on the lot with the most powerful engine, and insisted that it get 100 MPG, well, that's clearly someone you will never be able to please. If they are completely unrealistic in their expectations, you'd be better off cutting your losses sooner rather than later. You're not doing anyone, including yourself, any favors by promising more than you can deliver.

Remember, when working with a customer you need to be knowledgeable enough about both their business and the software that you are trying to sell in order to help them establish goals for themselves. For example, you might say to them, "I know that through the evaluation process you want to try to understand (fill in the blank). That's really great. However, I can also tell you that most people in executive positions above you are worried about (fill in the blank with something different) as well. Let's add this in so that you can then show it to them." Talk about making friends and influencing people! Your "stock" as a helpful professional in their eyes just doubled in an instant. This knowledge comes from doing your initial research, from talking with the prospect before the evaluation even begins, and "pre-seeding" the evaluation questionnaire with what you have gleaned from all of your homework.

Now you have the evaluator saying, "Hey, this guy really knows what he is talking about. These are good points. I'm going to fit them into my evaluation process." That's terrific, because you as the sales professional have now moved yourself from your own side of the table over to their side. You're now playing for the same team, removing any vestiges of an adversarial relationship and replacing it with a sense of moving together toward a shared goal. It becomes plain as day that both sides have a strong interest in achieving the same results.

Use Cases

These are situations where an evaluator wants to know how the software will work in various real-life applications at their company. For example, they might say that, as a user they want to see how a certain record will integrate into the new system, in order to prove that (if they go ahead and buy the software) the integration will work. Will it configure easily? These are practical demonstrations of how they would be using the software in their everyday business activities.

The beauty of this approach is that you can later go back to them and say, "We proved this use case, right? And this one, too? And this other one as well?" You get the idea. When they see how well the software performs the typical kinds of things that they will need it to do, that makes the decision to buy the software that much easier to make. What you are doing is reinforcing the need for them to have this product.

Moreover, you become an educator of how they should evaluate your system. This methodology allows you to do that because you are taking control. Each questionnaire will of course be different depending on the industry. And the more complicated the sale, the more complicated the questionnaire will be. For example, if you're dealing with the aerospace industry, and selling complex aerospace systems, they're going to get pretty complicated. That means there are more specific skills needed to sell specific things. This framework will undoubtedly work for any industry, yet at the same time a certain amount of customization will indeed be necessary.

Think of it this way. If we were trying to sell MS Word, we might ask, how many words a minute do you want to type? What page layout features are important to you? Those kinds of questions, which naturally would be quite different from the aerospace industry we had mentioned earlier. That's why it's important to find an area in which you excel and have an interest and to specialize in it. That makes you more highly sought after and therefore more valuable in the marketplace.

It's also important to implement *use case prompters*. These are questions that you ask that allow your customers to seed your questionnaire with the use cases that you want them to put in there. Of course, you need to be knowledgeable enough about the industry to be able to deliver that kind of information. These are questions where you already know the answers and you are trying to bring them along to the place where they themselves will actually say it. There may be one thing that is very important to your product compared to your competition. So you need to deliver this information to the customer, and educate them about it through this process so that they realize it and acknowledge that this is most definitely an important use case for them. They will then want to be sure that it is included in the evaluation. This is especially helpful if you already know that this is something that your competition will not be able to match.

If we were talking about cars, and the customer was looking at a two-seater, we might say, "You have three children, right? Won't you need something that you could drive them around in?" Then you point out that the vehicle that they've been looking at has a major drawback. They might want to consider something larger, perhaps an SUV, which is what you are selling. This rather obvious example is nonetheless an instance of employing a use case prompter. The best part of it is that you are getting the customer to bring up the point on their own by asking the right questions, seeding pertinent information and steering things in the right direction. You already knew what the answer was going to be, and you also knew that it was going to start making your competitor's product less attractive, while making what you are trying to sell that much more appealing to them. That is why this particular item would be something that ends up being included in the questionnaire.

With a well thought-out evaluation charter you maintain control of the process because all of the steps have already been laid out in advance. It's like an attorney who already knows the answers to the questions he is going to ask witnesses giving testimony. He would never ask a question without knowing the answer beforehand. Likewise, you know what your customer is looking for and how you are going to proceed at each point along the way. Dates have been agreed to for deep dive meetings, and once the process has begun, the use cases you demonstrate will show them that your product is a perfect match for their specific needs and requirements.

Be aware, however, that there will be times when you are in the middle of your charter, going through the evaluation, and the customer decides (or realizes) that there is something else that is not in the charter they want to see. Let them know that it's not a problem. Simply agree to it and add it to the charter and move forward. That's assuming it is something that you are able and willing to do. If not, just be diplomatic about it and say, "I'm sorry, but that's not something that we know how to, or are able to do, but let's move forward with what we already have in the charter." In other words, you need to make sure that you build in a certain amount of flexibility regarding items that were not in the charter initially. It is a framework, not an unchangeable, set-in-stone document that can never be tinkered with or altered in any way.

It's important to keep in mind that when people are evaluating something (it could literally be just about anything), they are asking to be educated. The salesperson, then, takes the role of an educator in a very real sense. Customers want to know what the product will do, how it will perform, etc. You should use the charter as a "course layout" and then the deep dives and the other things will constitute the actual coursework. In this way, you can see how the charter is almost like a syllabus for the entire evaluation process. It sets out in advance all of the important topics that are going to be covered, including a number of key details specifying exactly how each of them will be addressed.

4

Prove It!

The driving force behind all evaluations is to prove that you can do exactly what you claim that you can do with your products or services. The evaluation, therefore, provides a "guided" way to do that. It's about educating the customer regarding how this proof will be demonstrated to them. That's how we move the whole process forward.

Because you know in advance what your customers are looking for and what their concerns are (as outlined in the charter), you know exactly what it is that you need to bring to their attention. This is called a "deep dive" presentation, which takes things to the next level. It's a golden opportunity for you to prove to them things that you can't prove in a pilot or an evaluation or a trial. But you can accomplish it with this presentation, and knowing which deep dive to do is captured within your overall evaluation questionnaire.

This is where you want to be sure to ask what is called "trial acceptance questions." For example, you might say: "Based on what we've shown you at this deep dive meeting, will this handle what you've asked for?" The idea is to try to get the client to accept when working on a trial. If, for example, you were selling cars you might say to the customer: "So it was important to you that the car drives well in snow? Well, we took it out when it was coming down pretty hard a few days ago, and it handled really nicely. Did that satisfy your needs?" Of course, you already know and expect what the answer will be.

Accordingly, your charter would consist of all of the meetings that you want to have, including the deep dive presentations. These go into more depth of detail regarding a particular use case, things that would not likely surface during the normal evaluation process.

As you build out your charters, over time, you are learning more and more about what does and does not work. We compile all of this invaluable knowledge into what we call a playbook. Going back to the bedroom set scenario, we've determined that we need to do a deep dive presentation, down to even small details such as the tensile strength of the furniture, the quality of the glue that is used, the advanced nature of the bed's springs, etc. All of that information will go into your playbook for ongoing reference as new charters are drawn up for new sales that you are working on and trying to close.

Think about it this way. When someone initially downloads the product they have no idea how to determine for themselves whether or not it does precisely what they want. They need a system in place that will help to facilitate that, which is why the sales professional's role in the process is so crucial. Every sales tool – questionnaires, interviews with the customer, presentations – are geared toward helping the customer learn how to properly evaluate what is being pitched to them.

Otherwise, where else would they learn how to do this? There are no college classes that they can take in evaluation strategies. It is the sales person who must use the right strategy to demonstrate to them that the software fits the need that they want to solve. Remember, as mentioned earlier, in today's world they already know that they have the need. You don't have to tell them about it. Just realize that they are coming to you with needs they have already identified. Of course, they all expect that you will guide them in a systematic way through the process of convincing them that your product or service will suit their needs.

I've found that questionnaires are a particularly

effective tool. When you give someone a questionnaire, it means you have thought through the things that they will need to know to help them with their evaluation. I can't overestimate how important that is because it allows you to sell and position things that you might not be able to position directly and verbally. It's them answering the questions for themselves, which is decidedly better than you grilling them for answers, which, let's face it, can sometimes be a bit off-putting.

For example, I recall a company that we were selling to that wanted to evaluate our capabilities around requirements management. They hadn't thought about how important it was for them to have an election's process on requirements. But the questionnaire allowed us to "seed" information about an approval process for their requirements that was a feature of one of our products. However, you would have never gleaned that from any of our marketing collateral, even though it was a differentiator in the overall process that helped us to successfully prevail over our competition.

The salesperson had prompted the response, by stating in the questionnaire that some customers had asked about this particular issue, and was it important to them as well? As it turned out, it was, and that played a major role in closing the sale. We validated what they needed to know, and proved it through a deeper dive session, as described earlier.

What we are doing are raising issues that ultimately turn out to be important to the prospect, yet they may not have ever asked the questions if left on their own. It is crucial for our sales people to differentiate themselves as experts in the field, and then challenge our customers and prospects to look at things that they may need.

As mentioned previously, this is known as consultative selling. The questionnaire becomes the framework and guideline – you could actually think of it as more of an agreement between the two parties – before you start the evaluation. It leaves no ambiguity regarding what they are going to do and what we are going to do for them. It's the precursor for building an evaluation charter.

We've received some really encouraging feedback from our customers regarding the effectiveness of the questionnaires that we have them complete. It actually makes them think differently about the entire process and helps them in their ability to properly evaluate the project. In fact, we have had some of the evaluators thank us for our methods, because we make them look more successful in the eyes of their bosses.

We take all of the practices and techniques that

have helped in our sales efforts, and include all of them in what we call our playbook. It is very helpful for "seeding" ideas and overcoming objectives. It may even include all of the things that we do *not* do as part of our standard play when we are conducting an evaluation.

We also try to be anticipatory with our plays. For example, if the prospect says this, this and this (fill in the blanks), then we are going to do these things in a deep dive session (or some other tactic). The point is, having the playbook allows you to properly handle customers in a multitude of ways when they ask for certain things. You do this by running the plays that have proven to lead to success. As the name implies, it is rather similar to a football team's playbook that is filled with gridiron strategies that the team has successfully employed. It works in much the same way in the game of sales.

One of the standard plays that we like to use involves a customer asking us about the status of certain things, such as the status of integrating two systems. We don't want to acquiesce to that request, because it is too complicated and will make our product look rough. It also shortens the length of the evaluation process.

Of course, if the customer is adamant about it, then we use a different strategy: in that case, our best play is to go along with the request—but we get something in return. This is basically a negotiating tactic on our part, and again, it's part of the playbook for a very good reason: because it works.

On the other hand, I've also seen salespeople choose not to use the process, or use it rather loosely. The results are not pretty! It leads to lengthened sales cycles, causing us to not succeed in deals, and making our products look too complicated.

It's also important to remember that your playbook will be constantly evolving. It's not the Ten Commandments, given once and for all on some kind of stone tablet. On the contrary, think of your playbook as a way to document the tactics and strategies that, in a very real world sense, you and your colleagues have found to be effective and successful.

Products change. Situations change. That's why you have to have the right play for the right situation when you are on the field. In football, oftentimes the best plays are those that are called by the QB on the field right before the ball is snapped. The team recognizes that the game tends to be fluid, and therefore even the most solid game plan needs to have some flexibility built into it. The same thinking needs to prevail when you are playing the sales game.

5

Closing the Evaluation

Of course, closing the sale is our ultimate goal. We break it down into two types of closes, the technical close and the financial close. The technical close builds the emotion and want for the product. Financial closing is how they are going to pay for it. When you are trying to achieve the technical part of the closing, you go back over the charter and the questionnaire with the customer, reviewing the various areas that they had identified as important to them. You then ask the customer if all of their concerns were addressed adequately. Then you ask them if they felt that the evaluation was successful and if all of the hurdles were overcome, and if there is anything else other than financing that will prevent them from making the purchase. If they say no, their concerns were not adequately addressed, then you start all over again. If the answer is yes, then you ask them how they want to pay for it.

The whole idea is to bring the customer to the point where they are saying, yes, this is what we want, and this is something that will work well for us. Yes, it will be a good fit for our environment. Yes, this would be the best product for us to purchase. Getting the process to this point is the reason why we have both the questionnaire and the charter in the first place.

Everything that you have done so far has been leading to this meeting, the technical close. The charters, the deep dives, etc. – all of it – was carefully designed so that things will go very smoothly once you finally get here. You start by assessing the first "value point" for the customer. Have you effectively proven what you said you were going to prove through the process? Therefore, as you conduct this meeting you want to be sure to keep reaffirming this by asking the right questions. Has this satisfied your needs? Did we satisfy that use case during the process? If not, well then what percentage of the need was satisfied?

I think you get the point. This is the meeting where the customer ultimately agrees that they want your product or service. You have carefully tailored everything along the way to help them make this decision. It is quite literally the day of reckoning for the entire process. If you get to this meeting and the answer is no, then something is wrong. Somewhere along the way you messed something up. I know that may sound harsh, but in all truth it would be the only reasonable explanation.

You should know before going into the meeting exactly what the customer is going to say. Think of how an attorney in a courtroom already knows the answer to every question that he will pose long before he ever actually asks it. The closing scenario works in much the same way. Even the date of when this meeting will take place will have already been established, and codified in the charter, well in advance. For example: "We're going to evaluate for two weeks, we're going to evaluate these specific things, and we will wrap this up and conclude on this day and let's schedule that meeting right now."

Let's go back to that car dealership analogy one last time. The salesperson might say, "How did you like that car? Do you remember that we talked about how you wanted a sedan? Is this the sedan that you feel comfortable in?" If he or she is a good salesperson, they will already know the answers, because they have been asking the right questions to bring things to the point where the sale is going to be closed. (In like manner, of course, the right questions have been asked all along during the entire period that the customer has been evaluating the software.)

So what comes next? With the auto dealership, this would be when the salesperson asks, "So is there anything that would get in the way of you purchasing this car?" With software, it would be quite similar, perhaps, "Is there anything in the way of you moving forward with employing our software and getting value out of it?" The dealer might ask, "When would you like to take delivery of the car?" With software, the relevant question at this point would be, "When would you like to start the project?"

In the world of sales, this type of technical close is known as a "soft close." The "hard close" is always going to be the financial close when money comes in and papers and contracts are signed. This is when people finally take "ownership" of what you've been doing. The whole process is designed so that the technical influencers make the right recommendations (to buy your product!) and to, as we said, take ownership. This one meeting is what all of your hard work has been leading up to.

Many salespeople worry about objections, of course, so it's only natural that some may ask, what if at this late stage in the game I am still receiving objections? The best advice is to anticipate potential roadblocks well in advance and deal with them long before you ever get to the technical close. For example, whatever objections there may be should have come out during your deep dive meetings and you could have handled them then. In fact, that would have been the most appropriate time to do so.

Moreover, in your configuration sessions and other meetings when you are working with the prospect you should be driving toward this technical close, with all of the possible objections clearly in your mind, and overcome them now rather than waiting until later. Of course, if you do get an objection, hopefully by this point it would be a fairly minor one which you could get past by saying something such as, "Is this enough to stop you from moving forward with deployment?" This could help to distinguish an actual objection to buying the product from what may simply be a concern that you can swiftly allay for the customer before the close.

If the objection or concern sounds genuine, then you might ask, "OK, what can we do to prove that to you?"

If the answer comes back, "Well, I need more time to evaluate it," then you remain positive and reply, "No problem, how much more time do you need, and what can I do to help you through that?"

What you need to do at that point is to step back into a deep dive, and back into the framework or whatever else you need to do to prevent the entire process from sputtering to a halt. In this circumstance, you also must, almost automatically, re-do the conclusion meeting. We want to keep things as focused and specific as possible. What exactly is it that they would like to look at, or that they need to have proven to their satisfaction? Usually, however (if you've been following the charter!) these kinds of issues will have already been addressed far in advance.

Think of it this way, if you're not moving toward a technical close, you will already know that along the way. You will not hear about a problem for the first time at the very end of the process; you would have already learned of it much earlier. Long before the conclusion meeting—it could have been either during a checkpoint meeting or some other meeting—somewhere along the way these objections would have inevitably come out. Therefore, you want to be able to answer these objections satisfactorily before you have the confidence to ask, "Is there any technical reason why this wouldn't work for you in your environment?"

Of course, you are anticipating with near certainty that the answer will be no. You then follow-up with, "OK, let's get you into procurement…"

Typically, the conclusion meeting involves a bunch of different people, and not just your technical influencers. These are the people who you want to have say (about you), "This is a good product, they're a good company to work with. Look at the process that they used to help evaluate the software." This is a win for these individuals, because it makes them look good in their methodologies as well. Having them included is vitally important because they will play an invaluable role in effecting the end result.

When it comes to the financial close, these days nobody is going to write a procurement check until there has been a technical close on the software. That only makes sense when you think about it, because why would they even be talking about financial concerns if they have not yet been convinced from a technical standpoint that this is the right product for their company and their needs. That is why, unless there is a technical commitment that this is indeed what they want, you have not yet earned the right to ask for the financial close.

Once you are certain that they are ready for the financial close, only then can you say to them, "OK, I've already spoken with your procurement person. I've got your quotes all in line, is the exact number of users you're going to need, if so then let me go ahead and get our contracts done." Now you can see the light at the end of the tunnel. Sure, you have to be careful to dot all the I's and cross all of the T's, but by this juncture all of the hard work has already been done and the sale has become a foregone conclusion.

6

Wrapping It Up (the Benefits)

One of the key things that we can accomplish by using models in the right way is an improvement in the predictability of our pipelines. Because you are more effectively tracking your customers and tracking your evaluations, you know precisely where they are in the sales cycle. We are far beyond the days when a "model" was basically just handing over the software and saying, "here it is, try it out."

Under this new and far more refined approach, you have a much better idea, substantially earlier in the process, as to what the close ratio will be for the deals that you are currently working on. In many cases we have reduced the overall timeframe from months and years down to a matter of weeks. This is a truly dramatic turn of events that really can't be overstated.

All of this leads to more satisfied customers,

because they see how prepared you are and appreciate the level of professionalism in your organization. They remember what it took to get to the point of the technical close. At that point you will be able to ask the right key questions, such as, have we satisfied everything, and did the charter drive you through all the way to the end? The reply should almost certainly be in the affirmative. "We went through the entire evaluation, we were satisfied, and we will recommend your product to our stakeholders. We're ready to move on to procurement."

This is the goal of the whole process, and what you have been trying to make happen right from the beginning. You might be amazed by how efficient it is when it comes to solving problems. For example, I remember one situation where we had just finished running a pilot with a large multinational company. Their evaluation team was very complimentary of our evaluation process and the results, and they decided to buy our solution. An issue arose as we were the most expensive alternative and procurement pushed back. Fortunately, the credibility and goodwill we had built up with the business sponsors made this problem disappear almost as fast as it cropped up. We didn't even have to drop our price. The difference this made to us? Almost $1,000,000—on one deal.

Even better, once you have this new process in

place, it becomes repeatable and others can be trained to build upon the success that has already taken place. What you have now firmly established is a proven and very reliable sales model for taking your products to market. As we've mentioned earlier, to keep building on previous accomplishments, you develop different plays and different charters based on different scenarios. This allows you to execute each sales cycle in a repeatable way rather than operating in the dark each time.

The benefits to your management team are innumerable. For one thing, they will now have a better understanding of where the sale fits. Have we achieved a technical close? If so, then we can raise our ratio of success, which allows us to project where our pipeline is going to be, which also means we can project our revenue down the road.

All of this also gives management an opportunity to make better utilization of resources and time. That's always the case when you have the right framework and process in place. You don't have to waste time re-prepping every time you have a meeting. You know exactly what you're going to do in that meeting because you've done it before and it becomes more or less automatic.

This all gives you the ability to be sure that you are utilizing the right skills and the right people for each product. This plan that we call a charter also has the benefit of telling your customer precisely what you are going to do to earn their business. You can then bring in and allocate the right resources for selling this particular product with the help and co-operation of the customer. In other words, you let them become an integral part of selling themselves.

At this point, you've actually become much more than a relationship builder. Under this new approach, relationships are just a first step. In fact, you can even challenge your clients, asking them why they want to prove certain things. There is nothing confrontational about it. On the contrary, you are now working together as partners on this exploratory venture.

A "challenger" sales rep is a professional who will go to an organization and ask the right questions, do the right things, and challenge the prospects about how they will evaluate a new product. They do all of this in a way that will bring value to the customer. In fact, this is somebody who you would not hesitate to pay to come and talk to you because this person is capable of giving such great insight. They are more than just a sales rep, they are also a project manager and consultant who walks them through the steps of using your product.

The future of sales certainly seems to be moving in the "try it – buy it" direction, and that trend is showing every indication of continuing and strengthening. It's a far cry from just giving them the product and letting them guess. That's a reactionary sales approach and is fast becoming yesterday's news. The old "overcoming objections" model is no longer feasible in and of itself. The new, more interactive, highly co-operative strategy is much more in line with what customers want and expect in the modern business world.

Recommendations

If you are serious about building a successful and scalable enterprise sales organization you need your team to understand these principles and methodologies to achieve your growth objectives. The strategies and examples that Lance illustrates for you provide the building blocks you need to ensure your sales organization is productive as well as consistent with revenue targets and growth. The other invaluable benefit is that you will ensure your solution or software is implemented effectively for your customers to achieve their business goals. The result is a successful sales cycle that enables repeatable customer successes. It is a win-win for you and your company.

--William Nieporte COO

Lance and I used this methodology when we worked together, It allowed us to control the pilot process with defined dates and acceptance criteria. Bottom like my forecast was more timely and more accurate. This works.

--Stephen Turner EVP Sales

This Framework really accelerated my career as a Sales Engineer. As a new SE it provided the guidance I needed to quickly achieve the technical win and drive deals forward.

--Adam Jones: SR Sales Engineer

Strategies for Navigating the Technical Sale is a must read for anyone interested in proven strategies to win the technical close in a software sales engagement.

--Brian Ashcraft, Knowledge Architect Manager
Author, Jargonaut Express

This Framework really accelerated my career as a Sales Engineer. As a new SE it provided the guidance I needed to quickly achieve the technical win and drive deals forward.

--Jeff Down: SR Sales Engineer

www.ingramcontent.com/pod-product-compliance
Lightning Source LLC
Chambersburg PA
CBHW071631170526
45166CB00003B/1286